+

BEHIND THE BRAND

TIKTOK

BY SARA GREEN

BLASTOFF! DISCOVERY

BELLWETHER MEDIA • MINNEAPOLIS, MN

Blastoff! Discovery launches a new mission: reading to learn. Filled with facts and features, each book offers you an exciting new world to explore!

BLASTOFF! UNIVERSE

BLASTOFF! Beginners
GRADE K

BLASTOFF! READERS
GRADES 1-3

BLASTOFF! DISCOVERY
GRADE 4

This edition first published in 2024 by Bellwether Media, Inc.

Library of Congress Cataloging-in-Publication Data

LC record for TikTok available at: https://lccn.loc.gov/2023045256

Editor: Betsy Rathburn   Designer: Andrea Schneider

Printed in the United States of America, North Mankato, MN.

TABLE OF CONTENTS

FAMILY FUN!

A family wants to do a fun activity together. They decide to make a dance video for TikTok! They choose one of the latest dance trends. But first they must learn the moves!

A video on TikTok teaches everyone the steps. After some practice, the family knows the dance by heart. They set up a phone and take their places. Nobody makes any mistakes as they record. The video is sure to get many likes!

TIME FOR TIKTOK

TIKTOK HEADQUARTERS LOS ANGELES, CALIFORNIA

TikTok is a video-sharing **app** owned by a company called ByteDance. TikTok's **headquarters** are in Singapore and Los Angeles, California. TikTok's **logo** is recognized around the world. The app is available in more than 150 countries and 75 languages. TikTok has been downloaded more than 3 billion times!

TikTok users create and share videos up to 3 minutes long. Dance trends and entertainment are favorite topics. Sports, pranks, and educational videos are also popular. Today, the TikTok **brand** is worth around $66 billion!

A FLASHY LOGO

The TikTok logo looks like a music note. Its colors are designed to look like the flashy lights of a concert.

TIKTOK HEADQUARTERS

LOS ANGELES, CALIFORNIA

SINGAPORE

TikTok started in 2014 as a video app called Musical.ly. It was founded in China by Alex Zhu and Luyu Yang. Musical.ly's videos mainly focused on **lip-syncing**. The app quickly became a smash hit!

IN GOOD TIME

The earliest TikTok videos only lasted 15 seconds. TikTok expanded the time limit to 60 seconds in 2017. In 2021, TikTok allowed videos to last up to 3 minutes.

ALEX ZHU

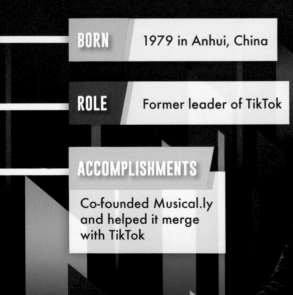

BORN   1979 in Anhui, China

ROLE   Former leader of TikTok

ACCOMPLISHMENTS

Co-founded Musical.ly and helped it merge with TikTok

BYTEDANCE OFFICE
BEIJING, CHINA

In 2017, ByteDance bought Musical.ly for around $1 billion. It also started a new app called TikTok. The following year, ByteDance **merged** Musical.ly with TikTok. The new app kept the TikTok name. TikTok was an instant hit. By 2019, the app had been downloaded more than one billion times!

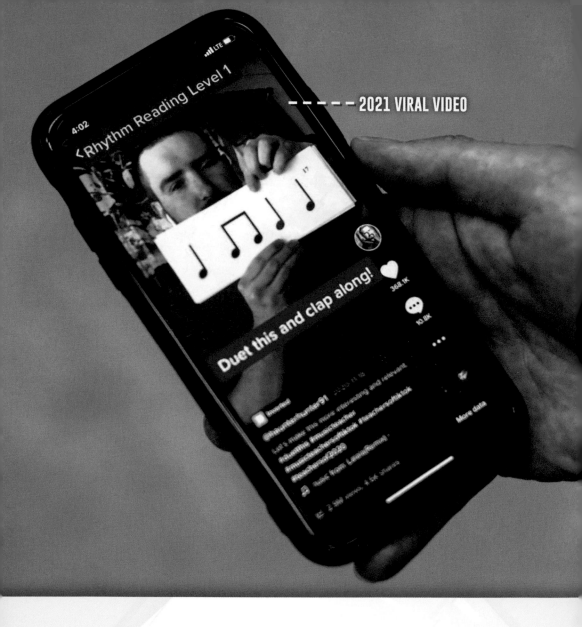

Trends on TikTok helped the app grow. People participated in challenges by making videos of themselves doing specific actions. The "no hands" challenge went **viral** in 2018. People recorded themselves holding their phones without using their hands. It was one of many viral videos to come!

Celebrities also joined in on challenges. Talk show host Jimmy Fallon started the tumbleweed challenge in 2018. He asked viewers to upload videos of themselves rolling like tumbleweeds. More than 8,000 people made videos. It was among the most popular challenges at the time!

SHOE CHANGE

The shoe change challenge was popular in 2018. People showed off different shoes and outfits to the beat of a song!

TUMBLEWEED CHALLENGE

JIMMY FALLON

Dance challenges also skyrocketed. One of the first to gain worldwide fame was the Renegade. It was created in 2019 by a 14-year-old dancer named Jalaiah Harmon.

ABOUT TIME!

Jalaiah Harmon did not get credit for inventing the Renegade dance until 2020.

EARLY TIKTOK DANCE TRENDS

FOOT SHAKE

Year It Went Viral: 2018

SAY SO

Year It Went Viral: 2019

GIT UP

Year It Went Viral: 2019

RENEGADE

Year It Went Viral: 2019

LAXED (SIREN BEAT)

Year It Went Viral: 2020

BLINDING LIGHTS

Year It Went Viral: 2020

CHARLI D'AMELIO

The Renegade quickly earned fans. One of them was a creator named Charli D'Amelio. She posted a video of herself doing the dance. Her video went viral, and Charli quickly became one of TikTok's top **influencers**. Millions of users posted videos of themselves doing the Renegade. This trend was one of many that helped TikTok grow. By 2021, the app had around one billion monthly users!

KHABY LAME

ADDISON RAE

Other creators helped TikTok grow. Addison Rae rose to fame in 2019. Her entertaining videos drew millions of followers. Today, more than 88 million people follow her. Khaby Lame started posting funny videos in 2020. Now, Khaby has around 162 million followers!

A song called "Laxed (Siren Beat)" went viral on TikTok in 2020. Over time, more than 55 million people have posted videos of themselves dancing to it. The song also led to the **Culture** Dance trend. People danced to the song while wearing clothes from their cultures.

CULTURE DANCE VIDEOS

TikTok's communities also draw in many people. Many creators enjoy sharing their favorite books. Videos in the BookTok community had more than 175 billion views by the end of 2023. BookTok has helped many authors find new readers!

BOOKTOK VIDEOS

NANA JOE

Fashion videos are also popular. Creators share their daily outfits, discuss new trends, and give fashion tips. Other creators enjoy sharing cooking content. They create videos of themselves making and enjoying their favorite recipes. Nana Joe is one of TikTok's top food influencers. She had more than 6 million followers in 2023!

FUN FEATURES

TikTok's many features help it grow. The For You page is a big reason the app is so successful. TikTok uses an **algorithm** to choose and post videos each user may like. The choices are based on what users have watched in the past. Everyone's page is different!

LIKE IT OR NOT

Liking videos makes TikTok's algorithm more likely to show similar videos. Clicking the "not interested" button tells the algorithm not to show similar videos.

Creators have many ways to make their videos stand out. They add sounds, music, filters, and special effects. Some **duet** with other videos to gain followers. **Hashtags** can also help videos get views. The best hashtags fit well with the content and are easy to remember.

Some TikTok creators earn money through their videos. The TikTok Creator Fund was launched in 2020. It rewards top creators for the number of views they receive. To qualify, creators must be 18 years or older. They must have at least 10,000 followers and 100,000 views within the past 30 days.

TOP TIKTOK INFLUENCERS IN 2023

KHABY LAME

Number of Followers:
162 million

CHARLI D'AMELIO

Number of Followers:
151 million

BELLA POARCH

Number of Followers:
93 million

ADDISON RAE

Number of Followers:
88 million

MR. BEAST

Number of Followers:
87 million

Creators can earn money in other ways, too. TikTok's Series feature debuted in 2023. It lets creators share special content. They earn money by charging their viewers a fee to watch certain videos.

BRAND DEALS

Some creators earn money by working with popular brands. Brands pay them to mention their products in videos.

TikTok finds ways to keep users safe. In most countries, TikTok users need to be 13 to use the full app. They cannot post videos or make comments. But they can watch kid-friendly content. This includes videos about building in *Minecraft*, making crafts, or having adventures with pets.

SCREEN TIME

TikTok has a 60-minute daily screen time limit for users younger than 18. This helps kids avoid spending too much time on the app.

TikTok will continue to grow. By 2025, the app may have more than two billion monthly users. They can look forward to new dances, challenges, and trends. TikTok's algorithm will continue to improve. Users will be able to find videos that are even more **personalized** to them!

FAMOUS TIKTOK PETS

OTIS	LOU	ROSIE	WINSTON	PINKY
TYPE OF ANIMAL: BOX TURTLE	TYPE OF ANIMAL: CAT	TYPE OF ANIMAL: GUINEA PIG	TYPE OF ANIMAL: SPIDER MONKEY	TYPE OF ANIMAL: PIG
NUMBER OF FOLLOWERS: 358,000 IN 2023	NUMBER OF FOLLOWERS: 249,000 IN 2023	NUMBER OF FOLLOWERS: 379,000 IN 2023	NUMBER OF FOLLOWERS: 2.3 BILLION IN 2023	NUMBER OF FOLLOWERS: 143,000 IN 2023

TikTok also faces challenges. TikTok's owner, ByteDance, began in China. Because of this, some nations worry that the app lets the Chinese government spy on their citizens.

GOVERNMENT MEETING ABOUT BANNING TIKTOK

PEOPLE SHOWING SUPPORT FOR TIKTOK

#KeepTikTok

TIKTOK TIMELINE

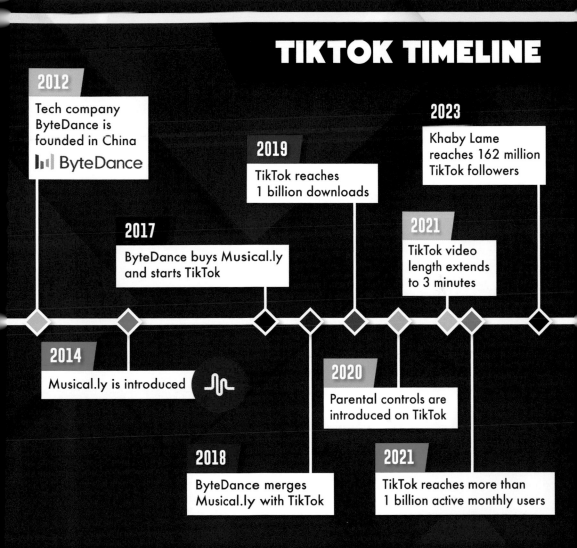

2012
Tech company ByteDance is founded in China

2014
Musical.ly is introduced

2017
ByteDance buys Musical.ly and starts TikTok

2018
ByteDance merges Musical.ly with TikTok

2019
TikTok reaches 1 billion downloads

2020
Parental controls are introduced on TikTok

2021
TikTok video length extends to 3 minutes

2021
TikTok reaches more than 1 billion active monthly users

2023
Khaby Lame reaches 162 million TikTok followers

In the United States, some leaders are trying to ban TikTok. Other countries have placed limits on the app. Canada and France do not allow TikTok to be downloaded onto government phones. Some countries such as India and Afghanistan have completely banned TikTok. In these countries and others, TikTok's future remains uncertain.

TIKTOK TEAMWORK

RED NOSE DAY EVENT

TikTok encourages people to help others. The company helps **charities** reach people and raise money for different causes. In 2019, the #ForClimate **campaign** helped teach people about **climate change**. More than 270,000 videos were made!

In 2023, TikTok gave $2 million to help business owners in Black and Latin communities. TikTok also participates in Red Nose Day. This yearly event raises money to help children. In 2023, TikTok gave more than $600,000!

GIVING BACK

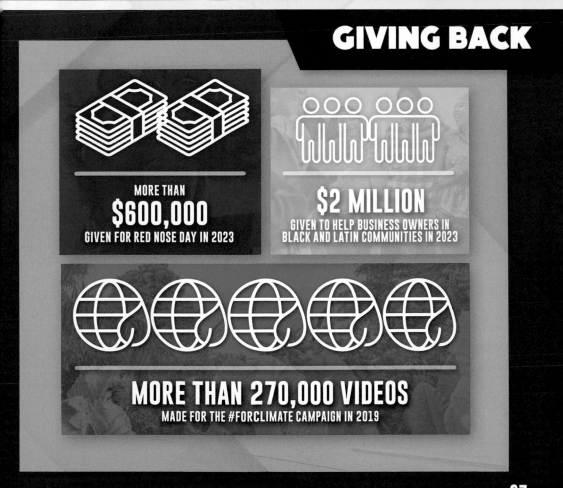

MORE THAN
$600,000
GIVEN FOR RED NOSE DAY IN 2023

$2 MILLION
GIVEN TO HELP BUSINESS OWNERS IN BLACK AND LATIN COMMUNITIES IN 2023

MORE THAN 270,000 VIDEOS
MADE FOR THE #FORCLIMATE CAMPAIGN IN 2019

TIKTOK TOGETHER!

TAYLOR SWIFT
CONCERT IN 2023

LIVE

LIVE STREAM

TikTok helps people come together in other ways. Some creators host **live streams**. Fans can see creators in real time, ask questions, and interact with other fans. Many TikTok users enjoy recording events to share with others. In 2023, many Taylor Swift fans did this to celebrate her popular concert tour!

Conventions also help TikTok fans come together. VidCon is the most popular video convention. In 2023, more than 50,000 people attended in person. Visitors meet TikTok creators and learn how to make videos. TikTok inspires creativity in people across the planet!

VIDCON

WHAT IS IT?

A convention for video content creators and their fans

WHEN IT HAPPENS — Yearly

FIRST HAPPENED — 2010

WHERE IT HAPPENS

Anaheim, California, and around the world

NUMBER OF ATTENDEES

More than 50,000 in person in 2023

GLOSSARY

algorithm—a set of step-by-step instructions that shows how to perform a specific task or to solve a specific problem

app—a program such as a game or internet browser; an app is also called an application.

brand—a category of products all made by the same company

campaign—a series of planned actions done to achieve certain goals

charities—organizations that help others in need

climate change—a human-caused change in Earth's weather due to warming temperatures

conventions—events where fans of a subject meet

culture—the beliefs, arts, and ways of life in a place or society

duet—to post a video alongside another creator's video

hashtags—words or phrases with the pound symbol in front of them; hashtags are used to put content into categories.

headquarters—a company's main offices

influencers—people on social media who can persuade their followers to do, buy, or use the same things that they do

lip-syncing—silently mouthing the words along with a song or other recording

live streams—events in which creators record themselves live

logo—a symbol or design that identifies a brand or product

merged—joined together

personalized—made to fit the needs of a specific person

viral—popular from being shared quickly

TO LEARN MORE

AT THE LIBRARY

Entrepreneur Kids. *All About Social Media*. Irvine, Calif.: Entrepreneur Press, 2021.

Green, Sara. *YouTube*. Minneapolis, Minn.: Bellwether Media, 2024.

Pearlman, Catherine. *First Phone: A Child's Guide to Digital Responsibility, Safety, and Etiquette*. New York, N.Y.: Penguin Random House, 2022.

ON THE WEB

FACTSURFER

Factsurfer.com gives you a safe, fun way to find more information.

1. Go to www.factsurfer.com.

2. Enter "TikTok" into the search box and click 🔍.

3. Select your book cover to see a list of related content.

INDEX